An Introduction to Computers

For Children – Ages 5 to 8 years

by

Dennis E. Adonis

Inside Illustrations by: Kristen Fogarty

Published by:
Learning Tree Media
Great Britain

Introduction to Computers for Children: - Ages 5 to 8 years

Learning Tree Publishers
West Sussex
Great Britain

Ordering Information:
For distribution details, please contact the publisher at:
info@learningtree.tk
www.learningtree.tk

First Printing, April 2012

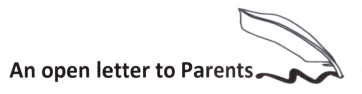

An open letter to Parents

Dear Parents,

You would acknowledge that children are much smarter and technologically adapted than us when we would have been there age not so long ago.

Kids are almost overnight experts at reprogramming our smartphones, the game box and most computerize gadgets than even their parents, most of the times.

Until a few years ago a book of this nature would have been inconceivable, since most parents would have thought that teaching a 5,6,7, or 8 year old the fundamental aspects of computers, as practically unnecessary for a child of that age.

Ironically, today we have no other choice but to accept that a child without computer knowledge, even as small as five years old, can encounter serious difficulties to adapt to a computerize school environment later on, and by extension, find it difficult reason effectively on such topics with children of his/ her age.

It is almost every good parent wish that there child receives nothing but the best that life has to offer, and in essence, the best education.

For every parent, the sooner their child can be drafted into understanding computer science, the better opportunities they may have for learning and adaptability down the road.

Therefore, in recognition of thousands of parents genuine desire to make their children computer educated from an early age, notable technology author and computer software engineer; Dennis Adonis has developed a methodology aimed at teaching children to better understand computers.

Teaming up with a team of some of the world's best children illustrators, he delivers technology learning in a child friendly and simplified scenario that is certain to help your child understand all of the important aspects of computers.

This book is the first of a three-part series, and deals with the technical situations involved in the setting up of a computer system, rather than the actual usage of a computer.

This strategy was taken because consultants and reputable educators agree that it may be in the child's best interest to first teach them the assembly aspects of computers, then progress to the usage and care categories.

Your decision to get a copy of this book for your child was certainly an excellent choice, and open evidence that you care about their academic development and future survival in a technologically advancing generation.

Learning Tree Publishing

Parental advice

Please note that based upon a prior two months test of this book contents, there were subsequent scenarios where children reading this book have assembled a desktop computer system and/or had taken initiatives to disassemble and reassemble a computer system.

While this may seem amusing and exciting to some parents, the Publishers and Author of this book wishes to advise parents against allowing this practice.

This book is intended to provide responsible education to children. Therefore, the Author or publisher would not hold themselves responsible for any child's action as a result of whatever they may have learnt from reading this book.

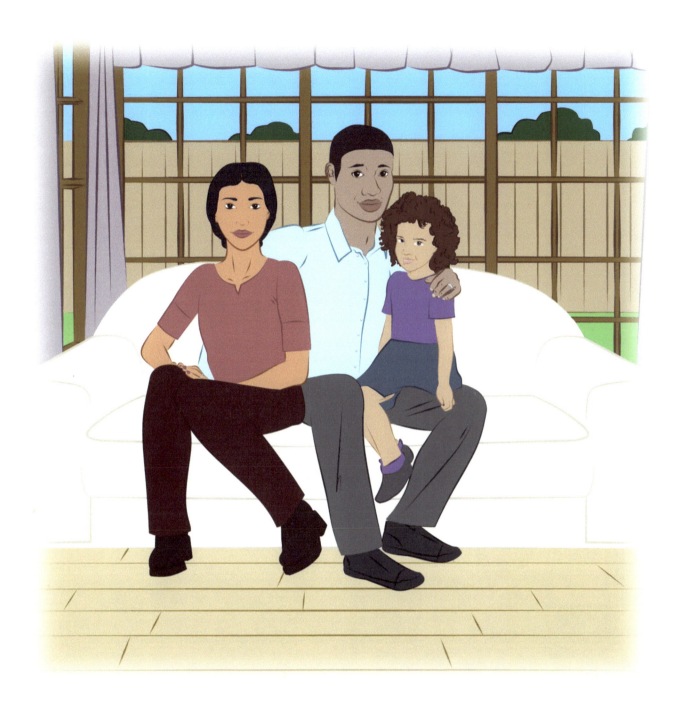

This is Mel. She is seven years old

Mel lives with her mom Sara, and her dad, Jim.

One day, Mel saw her Dad unpacking a large box which he had brought home.

Mel sat on the living room couch and watched at her dad from across the floor, as he unpacks items from the box.

First, her Dad unpacked a large object that looks like a small TV (television) screen.

Mel was excited, but wondered why her Dad had bought another TV set, when there was already one in the living room.

As she wondered upon the TV screen, her dad took out a tall rectangular shaped object which looked like a mini tower.

Her Dad placed the screen and the tall rectangular object on his work desk, then unpacked some wires and cables.

Mel cannot recall seeing so many wires and cables for a TV set, and posed a confused look on her face.

Her Dad noticed the look on her face, and decided to invite her over to where he was unpacking the objects.

Mel was happy that her Dad invited her for a closer look, and to tell her about the strange objects and what he was doing.

She quickly went over and sat on a small stool next to the desk, while her dad held up one of the wires, and told her, "I am putting a desktop computer together".

Mel was surprised, and told her Dad that she had first thought that it was another TV set. He smiled and told her that a desktop computer can indeed work like a TV set, but it also does more than a TV can do.

Her Dad then pointed his finger to the screen, and said, "This is called a computer monitor, computer screen or display".

Mel wondered at the strange words, and what a monitor or computer display unit does.

Her Dad then told her that it allows people to see pictures, words, videos and other things that the computer "brain" has to show them.

The kid was excited, but noticed that the computer monitor had some strange buttons at the bottom of its square frame.

Her Dad then pointed to the buttons and told her that the largest button is used to turn-on the computer monitor, while the other smaller buttons helps to make the screen brighter, darker, or changed for people whose eyes have special needs.

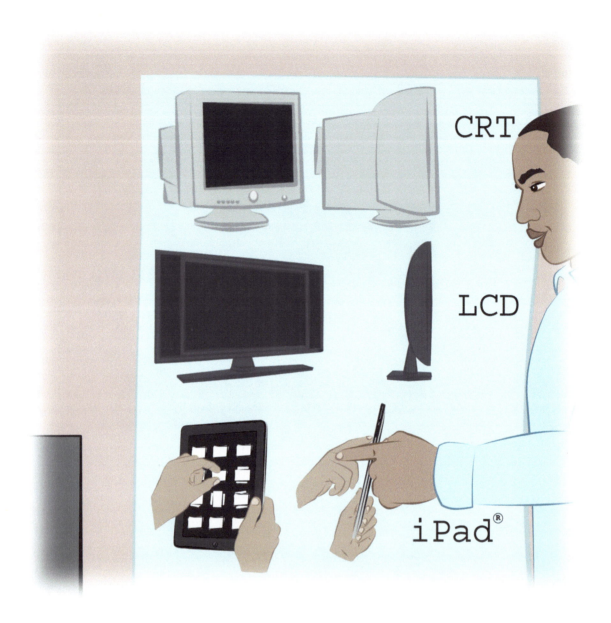

As her Dad spoke, Mel was certain that she had seen other monitors that seemed different from the one her Dad had unpacked. As such, she questioned him about other monitors. Her Dad smiled, then took a poster from the box, and showed Mel images of different types of computer monitors. He showed her monitors that have to be touched in order for people to use the computer, and others that people should not touch.

Mel then asked her Dad, "How does the computer monitor get pictures, words, and videos to show to people".

He patted Mel on her shoulder and said, "I will show you how".

"Just let me get some other items to explain it", he added.

Her Dad then took out a strange wire and told Mel that "this special wire is called a Video Cable or VGA cable".

He explain that it called a video cable because it is use to fetch videos, images and other information through it, which is taken to the computer screen (monitor).

He then plugged one end of the video cable into the back of the computer monitor.

The other end of the cable was then plugged into the back of the strange rectangular tower object that he had rest on the desk next to the screen.

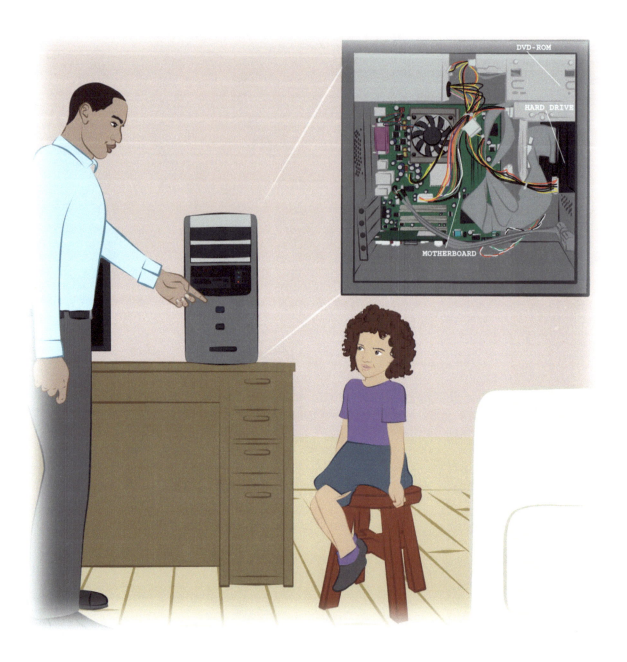

He told Mel that the tower object is called the "system unit" or the CPU (Central Processing Unit). He added that the unit is made up of several things inside the tower, including the CPU chip and a thick CD disk; - called the Hard Drive.

The Hard drive itself is like the brain which stores all of the pictures, videos and words on the computer.

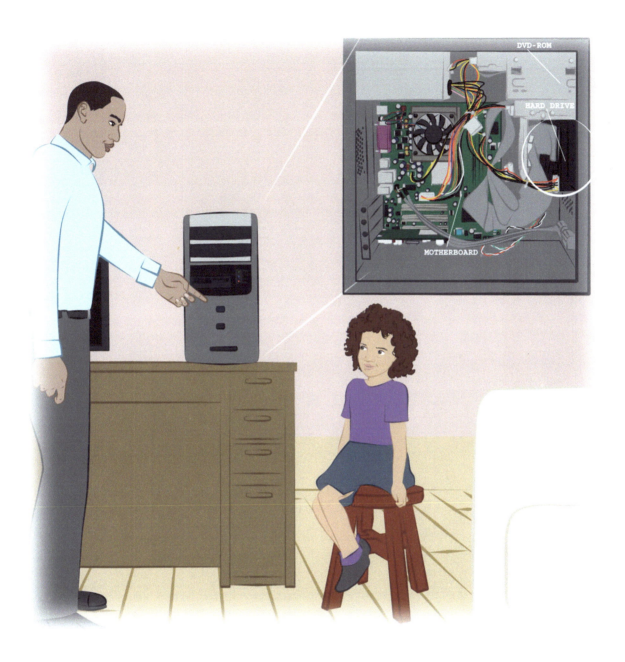

Mel learnt that the Hard Drive within the tower (or system unit) sends pictures, videos and other things through the VGA (video cable) cable to the computer monitor, so that people can see it. She also learnt that the hard drive and everything inside the "unit" are connected to a large chip, called the "mother board".

He carefully unpacked a flat rectangular object with lots of buttons on one side with a single wire at the back.

He then took the wire that dangle from the object and plugged it into the back of the tower (system unit), while placing it with the buttons face-up on the desk.

Mel learnt that the object is called a computer keyboard.
It is called a called a keyboard because it has lots of pressing
buttons called "keys', that are fitted on a flat surface that
shapes like a plastic "board".
The "keyboard" has keys of all the letters of the alphabet and all
the range of numbers from 0 to 9.
Her Dad added that the keyboard is used to type things and tell
the computer brain what to do. And whatever the keyboard
tells the computer to do, it will obey and show its reaction on
the monitor.

He also unpacked a second object with a strange semi-circle shape, and a wire leading out from it like a long tail.

The tail-end of the wire had a rounded shape which he plugged into the back of the system unit (CPU unit).

Mel was then told that the object is called a computer mouse; - this is because of its mouse shape and long-wired tail.

Like the keyboard, the mouse is used to tell the computer brain or CPU, what to do, or to choose and select things that you want to become active on the computer.

However, unlike the keyboard, you have to point to objects displayed on the monitor, and click them so that the computer can react.

Jim then took out two more black wires and told Mel that these are called electrical power cords.

He connected one of the cords to the back of the monitor, and plugged its other end into the power outlet on the wall.

Another power cord was plugged into the back of the CPU and the wall power outlet.

Mel's Dad then explained that in order for the computer to work, the monitor and CPU must have the right amount of electricity.

However, the keyboard and the mouse would receive small bits of electric current from the CPU, through the wires that are connected to it.

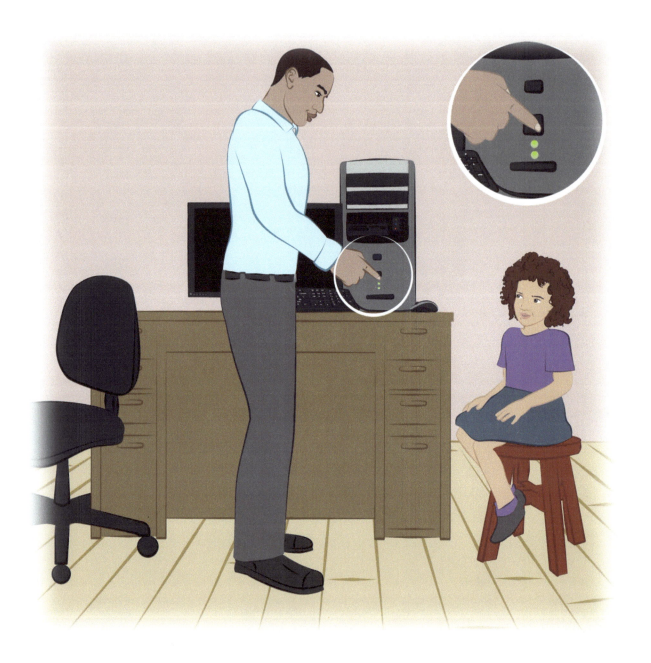

Jim then pressed the power button at the front of the CPU unit, and Mel could see two mini lights now blinking below the button, while a low humming sound was coming from the Tower.
Her Dad explained that the blinking lights and humming sound is a sign that the computer is starting up.

He also pressed the Power button in front of the monitor, after which the screen lighted up with several words and items flickering on and off. Jim explained that this is called the "booting" or "start-up" process of the computer, which always happens so that the computer brain or CPU can prepare itself to work.

A few seconds later, the computer screen stopped flickering and was now showing a background picture and lots of small objects across the screen with names such as "Office Word" below them. Mel learnt that it is called "the desktop", while the small objects on the screen (desktop) are called icons. A user can use the mouse to point and click on an icon to open files or access things.

Mel was glad that her Dad had told her so much about computers.

However, several grooves and holes on the computer's CPU made her question her Dad further on the reasons for them being there.

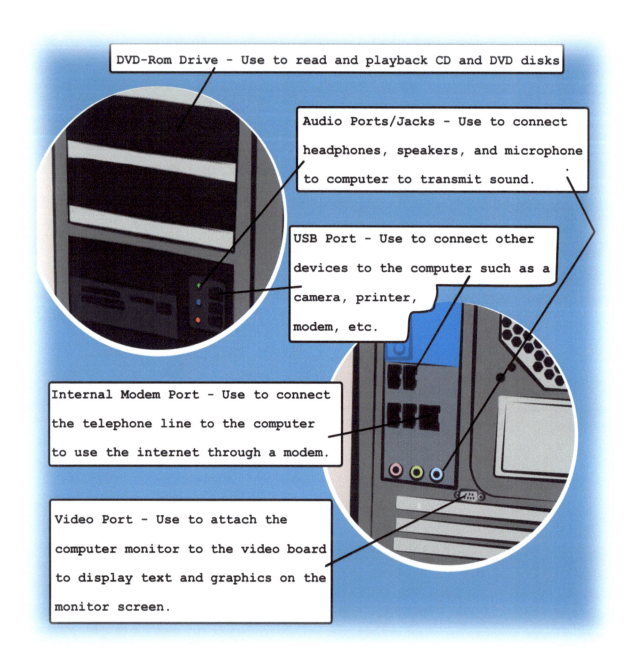

Jim smiled at Mel's interest and decided to tell her about the holes and grooves on the system unit (CPU unit).

He then pointed and carefully explained the purpose of each grove and port on the CPU unit.

To show Mel how important these holes and ports are, her dad decided to use a special cable and connect a printer to the computer CPU (system unit).

He then printed out pictures and other items that were being shown on the computer monitor.

A musical CD was also placed in the CD/ DVD tray, and a speaker was then connected so that Mel can listen to music and other sounds that were being played on the computer.

Mel enjoyed the music through her headphone and was surprise that the computer can also play CD's and DVD's.

Mel was happy and surprised at the many things that can be done with a computer.

She then asked her Dad if she can get a picture of Spongebob, Dora, or Spiderman from the computer.

Her Dad then told her yes, but the computer would have to be connected to the internet first so that it can find pictures and other things that are not on the computer hard drive (brain). He added that a computer hard drive (brain) does not always have all the things someone may need, because it would only have the things that someone puts into it.

Mel was glad to go on the internet to have many pictures and read stories about "Dora the Explorer".

However, her Dad told her that she would have access to all of her favourite cartoons when he connects the computer to the internet in a while, but she must eat her dinner first.

She giggled, hugged her Dad, and thanked him for his promise to find her favourite cartoons on the internet.

She then hurried off to dinner, as she was glad to know about the internet and the fun she can have on the new computer.

At the dinner table, her mom was sipping coffee and reading
from her laptop computer, while her dad joined them and
showed her mom a picture of the family on his iPad.
Mel did not see any unit (CPU tower) or connecting wires and
mouse dangling from the laptop or the iPad. She then asked her
Dad about the strangeness of his iPad and Mom's laptop.

Jim then explained that all computers have keyboards, hard drives, CPU's and so on. However, some computer parts are built smaller than others so that the PC can be carried around easily. He showed her the CD/ DVD drive, the monitor, and the keys on the laptop built-in keyboard that was all fitted together as one unit so that it can be carried around easily.

He also showed her the touch-screen keyboard on his iPad screen, and explained that in this case the keyboard and monitor operates together. But even though they may appear different in design, they all serve the same purpose, do the same things, and are all called; - computers.

The End

This has brought us to the end of this lesson. We encourage you to read volume #2 and volume #3 of this book to learn more about using a computer and the internet.

For further assistance, please write to us at: learningtree.uk@gmail.com

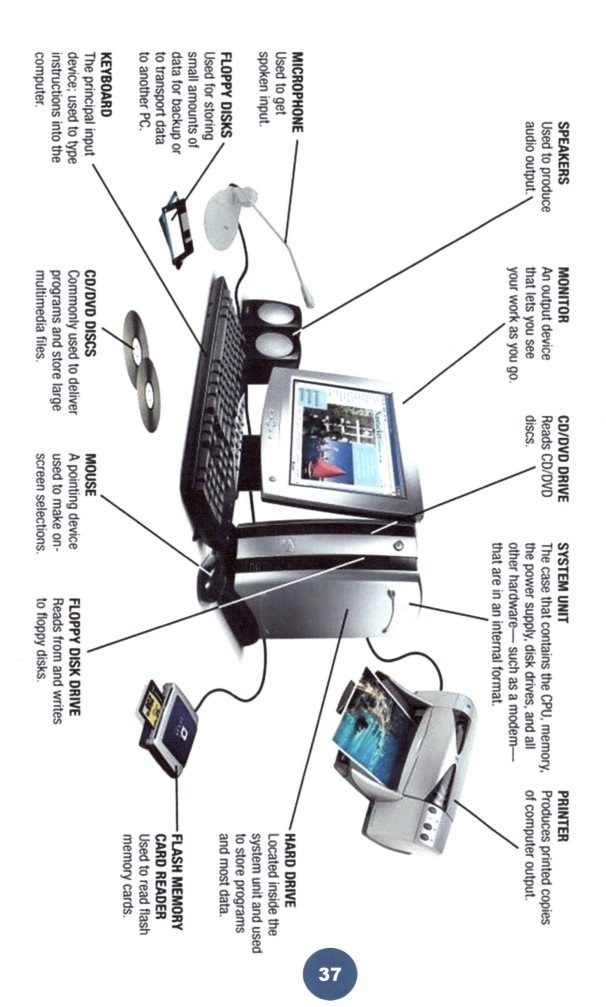

SPEAKERS
Used to produce audio output.

MONITOR
An output device that lets you see your work as you go.

CD/DVD DRIVE
Reads CD/DVD discs.

SYSTEM UNIT
The case that contains the CPU, memory, the power supply, disk drives, and all other hardware— such as a modem— that are in an internal format.

PRINTER
Produces printed copies of computer output.

MICROPHONE
Used to get spoken input.

FLOPPY DISKS
Used for storing small amounts of data for backup or to transport data to another PC.

KEYBOARD
The principal input device; used to type instructions into the computer.

CD/DVD DISCS
Commonly used to deliver programs and store large multimedia files.

MOUSE
A pointing device used to make on-screen selections.

FLOPPY DISK DRIVE
Reads from and writes to floppy disks.

FLASH MEMORY CARD READER
Used to read flash memory cards.

HARD DRIVE
Located inside the system unit and used to store programs and most data.

About the Author

Dennis E. Adonis is a prominent Guyanese Computer Software Engineer, Musician, Educational Author and Folk Novelist.

As of May 2012, he had written over a dozen books, half of which are based on Computer Science, including four children books in the same spirit as this one.

Mr. Adonis, himself a father of five adorable children, is known to be an excellent mentor and educator as it relates to helping children to understand the fundamental aspects of Information Technology regardless of their age grouping.

He had served as a mentor on many Children's computer teaching projects in the Caribbean and Europe, and had headed two *Unicef* assisted-projects aimed at teaching computers to children in his home country Guyana between 2005 and 2006.

His educational background in a variety of fields has also allowed him to be avail as a consultant for various entities over the years, but mostly as a Computer Security Software Engineer.

Outside of his work as an outstanding Author, he is currently a Contributing writer on Information Technology at Yahoo.com, and an *Adjunct* Curriculum Developer in Information Technology at Warnborough College, in England.

To interact with the Author, visit his Official Website at: **www.dennisadonis.net**

Author's Bio compiled by: Ms. Deon Brown
Learning Tree Publishing – Great Britain.

www.ingramcontent.com/pod-product-compliance
Lightning Source LLC
Chambersburg PA
CBHW041424050326

40689CB00002B/643